X-treme DISASTERS
THAT CHANGED AMERICA

EARTHQUAKE!

The 1906 San Francisco Nightmare

by Lynn Brunelle

Consultant: Daniel H. Franck, Ph.D.

BEARPORT
PUBLISHING COMPANY, INC.

New York, New York

Credits

Cover, Library of Congress Prints & Photographs Collection.
Title page, Library of Congress Prints & Photographs Collection; 4, Library of Congress Prints
& Photographs Collection; 5, Roy D. Graves Pictorial Collection, Bancroft Library, University of
California, Berkeley; 6-7, 7(inset), Underwood Archives; 8, CORBIS; 9, 10-11, Underwood Archives;
12-13, Louis Pappas and Monica Ponomarev; 15, Bernhard Edmaier / Science Photo Library / Photo
Researchers, Inc.; 16, AP Photo / Francesco Bellini; 17, James King-Holmes / Photo Researchers,
Inc.; 18, PictureQuest; 20-21, 21(inset), Underwood Archives; 22, Library of Congress Prints &
Photographs Collection; 23, CORBIS; 24, AP Photo / John Swart; 25, AP Photo / Paul Sakuma; 26,
AP Photo / The Sun, Larry Steagall; 27, Courtesy of Nitro-Pak Preparedness Center, www.nitro-pak,
800.866.4876; 29, Jim Sugar / CORBIS.

Design and production by Dawn Beard Creative, Triesta Hall of Blu-Design,
and Octavo Design and Production, Inc.

Library of Congress Cataloging-in-Publication Data

Brunelle, Lynn.
 Earthquake! : the 1906 San Francisco nightmare / by Lynn Brunelle ; consultant, Daniel H. Franck.
   p. cm. — (X-treme disasters that changed America)
 Includes bibliographical references and index.
 ISBN 1-59716-008-3 (lib. bdg.)—ISBN 1-59716-031-8 (pbk.)
 1. Earthquakes—California—San Francisco—Juvenile literature. 2. Fires—California—San
Francisco—Juvenile literature. I. Title. II. Series.

 QE535.2.U6B78 2005
 363.34'95'0979461—dc22

                    2004020743

For more information, write to Bearport Publishing Company, Inc., 101 Fifth Avenue, Suite 6R, New
York, New York 10003. Printed in the United States of America.

 3 4 5 6 7 8 9 10

Table of Contents

Shaking at Dawn

On April 18, 1906, the sun had just begun to rise in San Francisco, California. Most people were asleep. Others were getting ready for work.

Thomas Jefferson Chase was a ticket **clerk** on a ferryboat. As he walked to his job, the streets were empty and quiet. Suddenly, without warning, a loud roar and **rumble** filled the air. The ground shook so hard that Thomas was thrown flat on his face.

◀ San Francisco, California, before the earthquake of 1906

The ground kept shaking. Then it opened up around him. He couldn't stand up.

What was going on? A huge **earthquake** was happening. It would change San Francisco forever.

▼ San Francisco, California, after the earthquake of 1906

The noise heard during an earthquake is the sound of the earth moving and buildings being shaken.

Broken Windows, Broken Lives

Nearby, young Lloyd Head held onto his shaking bed so he wouldn't fall out. The house was rocking back and forth. When the shaking stopped, he ran to his parents' room. The whole family looked outside.

▼ The 1906 San Francisco Earthquake caused fires to break out all over the city.

Buildings had fallen down. Windows were broken. There were huge holes in the earth. The sidewalks were cracked and bent. Water flowed from pipes that had burst. Crowds of people were on the streets.

Downtown, Lloyd could see a fire. He didn't know it, but gas was coming out of broken gas lines all over the city. The real **terror** was just starting.

San Francisco is in northern California. Earthquakes also occur in southern California. About 10,000 small earthquakes occur there each year.

Fire!

Thomas Chase had stayed away from flying stones and sparking power lines to get to work. Now he helped people onto ferryboats.

The gas had caught fire and flames covered the city. Horses couldn't get through the broken streets. Firefighters had to get to the fires on foot. When they reached a fire there was no water to put it out. The pipes had burst.

▲ The fires burned for four days. Firemen, along with thousands of volunteers, worked around the clock to put out the flames.

Lloyd Head's mother sewed bags together to make a tent. The family camped outside. They were afraid their house would fall. People watched rescue workers try to put out the flames with coats and brooms.

▲ This San Francisco street cracked during the powerful earthquake.

Soldiers blew up buildings to stop the fire from spreading.

A Shattered City

Three days later, the fire was out. The shaking had stopped. The beautiful city of San Francisco was a mess.

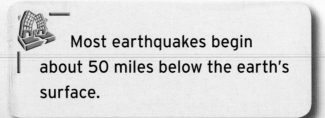

Most earthquakes begin about 50 miles below the earth's surface.

The death count was about 700. People who study history, however, say as many as 3,000 people died. About 225,000 people were hurt. The earthquake **destroyed** 490 city blocks. Over 25,000 buildings had fallen. It would take millions of dollars to rebuild San Francisco.

Without warning, much of San Francisco had been flattened like a sand castle hit by a wave. How did it happen? How does any earthquake happen?

What Is an Earthquake?

The city had been hit by shock waves. These waves start below the earth's surface, where there are large pieces of rock. These rocks are called **tectonic** (tek-TAHN-ik) **plates**. The plates fit against one another like a puzzle.

Each plate floats on hot liquid rock. Sometimes plates push against each other. If the plates slip while they're pushing, shock waves occur. These waves travel up and can cause the ground to move.

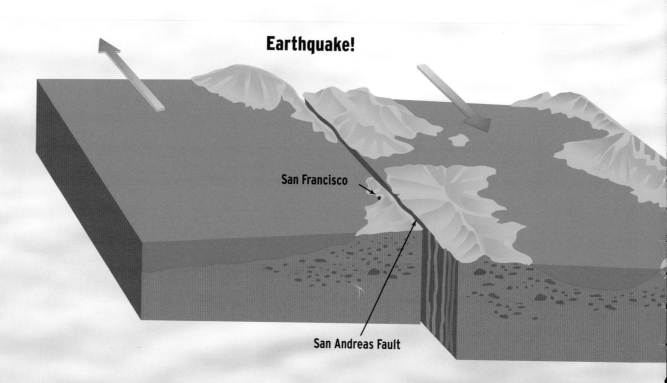

Earthquake!

San Francisco

San Andreas Fault

An earthquake is caused by movements within the earth's crust.

An earthquake is usually followed by **aftershocks**. The aftershocks occur as the rocks get into their new positions. The 1906 San Francisco Earthquake had 135 aftershocks.

Inside the Earth

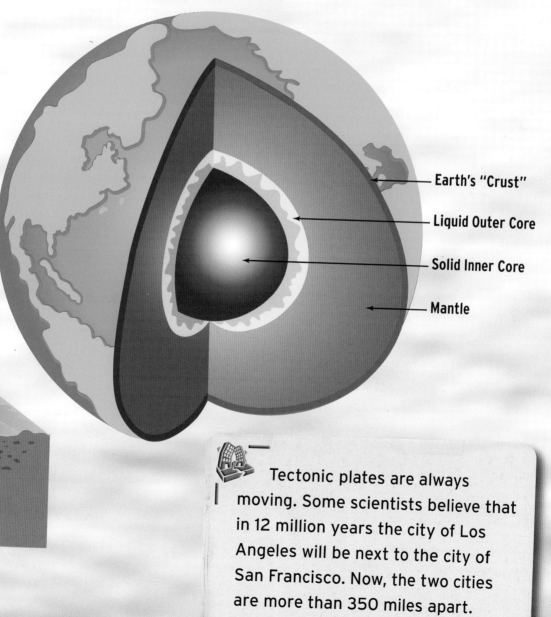

Earth's "Crust"

Liquid Outer Core

Solid Inner Core

Mantle

Tectonic plates are always moving. Some scientists believe that in 12 million years the city of Los Angeles will be next to the city of San Francisco. Now, the two cities are more than 350 miles apart.

Whose Fault Is It?

Each year, half a million earthquakes occur around the world. Most are harmless. About a hundred are big enough to cause trouble, mainly those near cities.

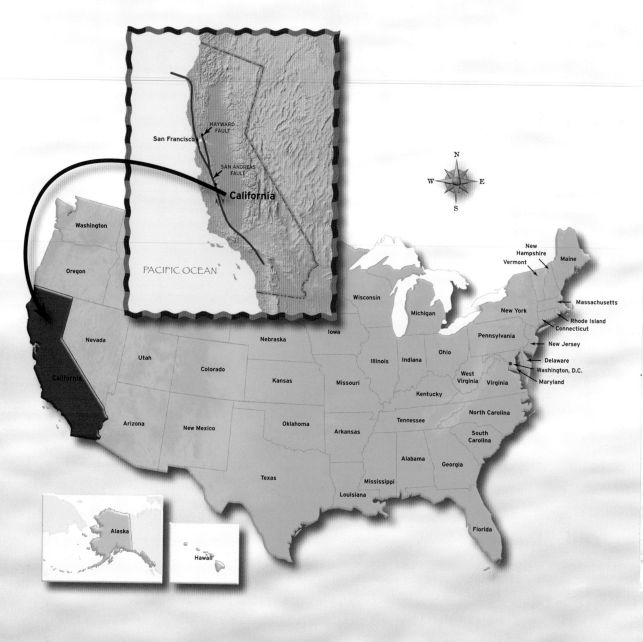

Earthquakes usually occur along weak places in the earth's **crust** called **faults**. San Francisco sits on the San Andreas Fault. This fault stretches along part of the state. It causes most of California's many earthquakes.

◀ The San Andreas Fault in California

Another large fault in California is the Hayward Fault.

Take a Number

Since 1906, scientists have learned a lot about earthquakes. They have special tools to help them. One is a seismograph (SIZE-muh-*graf*). It's used to record the movement of the earth during an earthquake.

▲ A scientist looks at a chart from a seismograph after an earthquake hit Italy in 1997.

Scientists give each earthquake a number on the Richter (RIK-ter) Scale. This scale measures the power of an earthquake. The highest numbers go to the biggest earthquakes.

The scale uses numbers and parts of numbers to measure power exactly. If an earthquake is rated "five point two," that means its number is 5.2. It has more power than an earthquake rated 5.1.

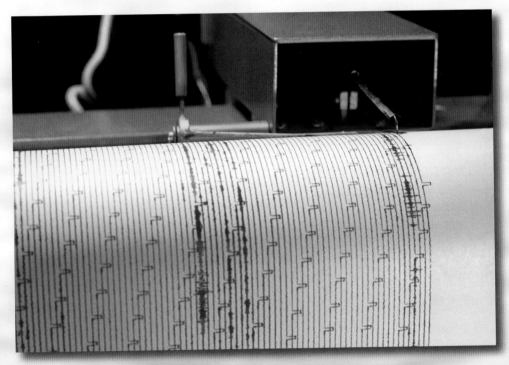

▲ Movements of the earth show up as heavy lines on a seismograph chart.

The biggest earthquake in the world measured 9.5 on the Richter Scale. This earthquake occurred in Chile in 1960.

America's Biggest Shake-ups

The 1906 San Francisco Earthquake wasn't the biggest earthquake to ever occur. It was, however, the most harmful earthquake in American history.

▲ The Golden Gate Bridge in San Francisco, California

It caused so much damage because it hit a big city with lots of buildings and people. Earthquakes that hit places with few people and buildings don't cause as much harm, even if they have more power.

America's 10 Strongest Earthquakes on Record*			
Rank	Location	Date	Magnitude
1	Prince William Sound, Alaska	March 28, 1964	9.2
2	Andreanof Islands, Alaska	March 9, 1957	9.1
3	Rat Islands, Alaska	February 4, 1965	8.7
4	East of Shumagin Islands, Alaska	November 10, 1938	8.2
5	New Madrid, Missouri	December 16, 1811	8.1
6	Yakutat Bay, Alaska	September 10, 1899	8.0
7	Andreanof Islands, Alaska	May 7, 1986	8.0
8	New Madrid, Missouri	February 7, 1812	8.0
9	(Near) Cape Yakataga, Alaska	September 4, 1899	7.9
10	Fort Tejon, California	January 9, 1857	7.9

* From the United States Geological Survey

The San Francisco Earthquake of 1906 would be number 17 on this list. It hit the Richter Scale at 7.8.

Looking for Clues

Days later, Thomas Chase was safe at his mother's house in Oakland, California. Lloyd Head's family was still camping outside. Thousands of others were in tents in the city's parks. They hung signs with names like "Camp Thankful." They were glad to be alive.

Scientists studied photos and maps of the places hit. Workers hunted through the fallen buildings and homes. They were looking for ideas to help make a safer city. They found that buildings on soft land were damaged more than buildings on solid rock. They learned the fire had caused more problems than the earthquake.

◀ A family that lost their home during the earthquake

The moon also has "earthquakes." These "earthquakes" don't happen often and they aren't strong.

A New San Francisco

After the earthquake, the city made new building rules. The rules were very tough for buildings on soft ground. Tall buildings were made to move with earthquake shocks instead of falling to pieces. Most new buildings had to have steel frames.

New water pipes that could bend easily were put to use. These pipes would be less likely to burst. New gas lines were made more bendable, too.

▲ By 1910, many buildings in San Francisco had been rebuilt.

San Francisco did not put these new rules into effect all at once. The city, however, was ready to welcome visitors to the 1915 World's Fair.

◀ A poster from the 1915 World's Fair

The tectonic plates along the San Andreas Fault slide against each other about as slowly as a fingernail grows.

San Francisco Hit Again!

In 1989, another large earthquake shook the city. One place it hit was San Francisco's Candlestick Park. It was before the start of a World Series game. Millions of Americans watched on TV.

▲ A damaged building being torn down after an earthquake in San Francisco in 1989

This earthquake measured 6.9 on the Richter Scale. This time the city was more prepared. Buildings shook but most did not fall. There was, however, some damage. Parts of the San Francisco-Oakland Bay Bridge fell. A section of the freeway in Oakland fell, too. Forty-two people were killed. Power was knocked out. Fires started around the city. Again, the most damage happened to buildings on soft land.

▼ Workers check the damage to the freeway in Oakland after the earthquake in 1989.

Damage from the 1989 earthquake cost about 6 billion dollars.

The Future

Scientists think another big earthquake might strike San Francisco in the next 30 years. More than 1,000 earthquake stations are on the lookout for shock waves along California's fault lines. If it seems like an earthquake is about to happen, people can be warned. Families have **emergency** supplies of food and water. Kids in school practice safety moves such as hiding under a strong table.

▲ A teacher and a student during a school earthquake drill

Earthquake study in America began because of the 1906 San Francisco Earthquake. Now we know much more. We can't stop an earthquake, but we can live through one.

▲ An earthquake survival kit

 Every year about 500,000 earthquakes occur. Only about 100 cause damage.

Just the Facts

The San Francisco Earthquake of 1906

- The first shock of the San Francisco earthquake hit at 5:12 a.m. on April 18, 1906. It lasted 48 seconds. Some of the 135 aftershocks lasted as long as 45 to 60 seconds.

- The center of the earthquake was near San Francisco. The earthquake, however, could be felt from Los Angeles all the way up to Oregon.

- The fire was as harmful as the earthquake. Many people now call the **disaster** the Great Fire and Earthquake of 1906.

All About Earthquakes

- Alaska has more earthquakes than any other state. California has the second most earthquakes.

- Florida and North Dakota have the fewest earthquakes.

- About 70% of all earthquakes happen around the edges of the Pacific Ocean. This area is called the "Ring of Fire."

- Most volcanoes occur in the "Ring of Fire," too.

- The earthquake that killed the most people happened in the year 1201, near Egypt. More than a million people died.

Earthquakes Today

- More than 1,000 centers in California have seismographs to watch for earthquakes.
- New building rules make highways and buildings safer during earthquakes.
- Scientists have studied where earthquakes occur. They have made maps so cities can decide where the safest places are to build schools, hospitals, and homes.

▲ The Cypress Freeway, at dawn, after the 1989 earthquake in San Francisco

Glossary

aftershocks (AF-tuhr-*shoks*)   earthquakes that come shortly after a bigger earthquake in the same area

clerk (CLURK)   person who sells things in a store

crust (kruhst)   the hard outer layer of the earth

destroyed (di-STROID)   ruined completely

disaster (duh-ZASS-tur)   something that happens suddenly and causes much damage or loss

earthquake (URTH-*kwayk*)   a sudden shaking of a part of the earth, caused by movement of the earth's crust

emergency (i-MUR-juhn-see)   related to a sudden situation that must be dealt with immediately

faults (FAWLTS)   large cracks in the earth's crust

rumble (RUHM-buhl)   a low heavy rolling sound

tectonic plates (tek-TAHN-ik PLAYTS)   sheets of rock that make up the earth's outer crust

terror (TER-uh)   something that causes great fear

Bibliography

Moores, Eldridge M. Dr., Editor. *Volcanoes and Earthquakes.* New York, NY: Time–Life Books (1995).

Silver, Donald M., Ph.D. *Earth: The Ever-Changing Planet.* New York, NY: Random House Library of Knowledge (1989).

Read More

Mehta-Jones, Shilpa. *Earthquake Alert!* New York, NY: Crabtree Publishing Company (2004).

Osborne, Mary Pope. *Earthquake in the Early Morning* (Magic Tree House). New York, NY: Random House Children's Books (2001).

Learn More Online

Visit these Web sites to learn more about earthquakes:

http://earthquake.usgs.gov

http://www.fema.gov/hazards/earthquakes

http://www.sfmuseum.org/1906/06.html

http://www.worldhistory.com/wiki/1/1906-San-Francisco-earthquake.htm

Index

About the Author

Lynn Brunelle is an Emmy Award-winning writer and illustrator. She lives in Seattle with her husband and two young sons.